D0768905

SNOWMOBILE
Bombardier's Dream Machine

Jules Older • ***Illustrated by*** **Michael Lauritano**

Charlesbridge

Published by Charlesbridge
85 Main Street
Watertown, MA 02472
(617) 926-0329
www.charlesbridge.com

Jules Older gives 10% of his profits from his kids' books to people who help kids. This time the money goes to Water.org, which brings clean, safe drinking water to some of the poorest kids on Earth. Check 'em out for yourself at **www.water.org**.

Library of Congress Cataloging-in-Publication Data
Older, Jules.
Snowmobile : Bombardier's dream machine / Jules Older.
p. cm.
Includes bibliographical references and index.
ISBN 978-1-58089-334-3 (reinforced for library use)
ISBN 978-1-58089-335-0 (softcover)
1. Snowmobiling—Juvenile literature. 2. Snowmobiles—Juvenile literature. I. Title.
GV850.5.O54 2012
796.94—dc22 2011000810

Printed in China
(hc) 10 9 8 7 6 5 4 3 2 1
(sc) 10 9 8 7 6 5 4 3 2 1

Illustrations done in Sumi ink and grease pencil on Bristol board
Display type and text type set in Coldsmith and Adobe Garamond Pro
Color separations by Jade Productions
Printed and bound September 2011 by Jade Productions in Heyuan, Guangdong, China
Production supervision by Brian G. Walker
Designed by Diane M. Earley

To our growing family
The Originals: Effin, Amber, and Willow
The Newbies: Leroy, Max, Ben, and Asher

—J. O.

For my parents, who have always supported my ambitious dreams, however uncommon or impractical

—M. L.

Merci Plenti
A lot of kind people, many of them from Quebec, helped keep *Snowmobile* real. Here are the kindest of all . . . Patrick Leith and Anne-Marie Fleet for help with All Things French; Brian Puddington for the feel of old Montreal; the Bombardier family and the J. Armand Bombardier Museum for all kinds of details about the life of Joseph-Armand and the invention of the Ski-Doo®* snowmobile; Effin Older for home editing, proofreading, encouragement, and reality checking. Reality checking? "That is the dumbest sentence in the history of the English language."; and most especially, my longtime friend and editor at Charlesbridge, Randi Rivers. Randi thought big when I thought small, thought accurate when I thought lazy, and actually found a way to describe what difference a cog makes . . . that didn't put readers to sleep.

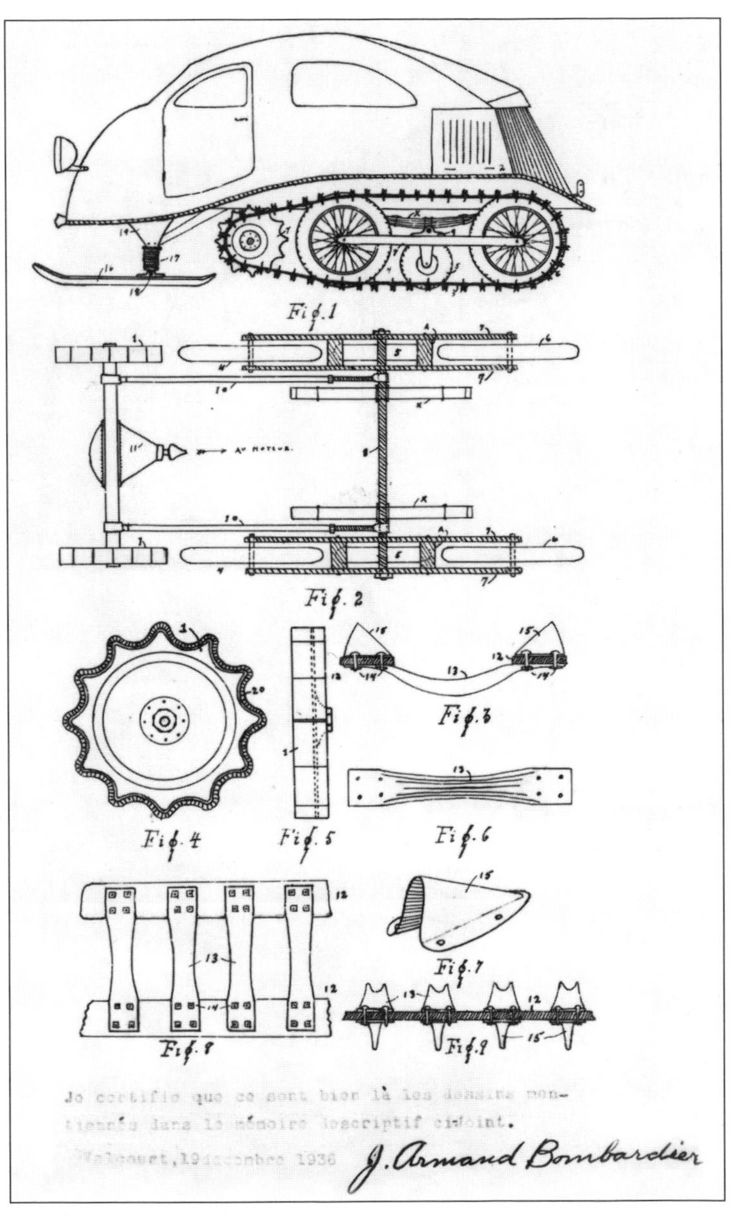

Joseph-Armand Bombardier's first patent, issued in 1937, for his sprocket wheel/track system.

TABLE OF CONTENTS

Yvonne put her arms around
him and kissed him tenderly.
"You invent things, *mon cher.*
Ours is not the only child who
cannot get to a hospital in winter.
Now stop pacing and go invent
something that will go on snow."

Chapter I

DEATH HANGS IN THE AIR

Cold. Night. Snow. And death hangs in the air.

Downstairs, Joseph-Armand Bombardier paced. And paced.

Upstairs, Yvon, his two-year-old son, lay hot with fever. Beside his crib sat the boy's mother, Yvonne. Her sisters huddled around her and the crib. They took turns wiping Yvon's forehead with cool cloths.

They'd all been there for hours, yet Yvon was no better. If anything, he was worse.

As time passed Yvon's fever grew hotter. His cries were now sad whimpers. His color was slowly fading from

fevered red to pale white—the same color as the Quebec snow that blanketed the house, the barn, the village.

Yvonne sighed. "I must get more water." The other women nodded. They knew she needed a break more than the water bowl needed refreshing. "Go, Yvonne. We'll watch over Yvon."

Yvonne paused halfway down the wooden staircase. She held back a sob.

There in the parlor Joseph-Armand paced the floor, just as he had when she'd last refilled the water bowl an hour before, and the hours before that. Only now he muttered, "If only we could get him to a hospital. . . . If only we could get him to a hospital. . . ."

Yvonne descended the last of the stairs, set the bowl on the pine washstand, and lightly touched her husband's arm. Her touch stopped his pacing. "Yvonne! The snow is too deep. . . . I can't . . . I . . ."

"I know, Joseph-Armand. You can't get Yvon to the hospital, just as I can't get his fever down. That's simply the way it is." Yvonne wiped her eyes on the sleeve of her blouse. She steadied herself with a deep breath. "If it is God's will, Joseph-Armand, then—"

Joseph-Armand shook loose from her touch. "*Non! Non,* Yvonne!"

She pulled back, shocked by his fierce reaction.

"Joseph-Armand, I was just—"

Now it was Joseph-Armand who sighed. "I know, I know. You are a good wife, Yvonne. And a good Catholic woman. I try to be a good Catholic, too."

He inhaled deeply. "The ways of God are mysterious, but there is one thing I know for certain: God did not intend for our child to die because we—no, because *I*—cannot figure out how to do something as simple as *drive through snow. . . .*"

"Joseph-Armand, stop this—"

"No, Yvonne. This is not God's will. This is *my* failure."

Her eyes filled with tears, and Yvonne once again took Joseph-Armand's arm. "Dear husband, you may not have discovered how to drive over snow, but neither has anyone else in Quebec. Nor in Canada. Nor in the entire world. So please, stop blaming yourself. Get back to what you do best, while I do the same."

Joseph-Armand attempted a smile. "My dear Yvonne, you are the best mother in the world. But right now I cannot think of a single thing that I can do."

Yvonne put her arms around him and kissed him tenderly. "You invent things, *mon cher.* Ours is not the only child who cannot get to a hospital in winter. Now stop pacing and go invent something that will go on snow."

CHAPTER 2
THINGS GO BANG

Long before he was a father, Joseph-Armand Bombardier had two passions. The first was motors.

Joseph-Armand was born in the country village of Valcourt in the Canadian province of Quebec in 1907. At that time the motor—when used to propel a wheeled vehicle—was as new and exciting as iPads and iPhone apps are today. The first patent for an automobile was granted in 1886 in Germany, but it wasn't until 1901 that a man named Ransom Olds in the United States started mass-producing cars—he called them Oldsmobiles.

And it was not until 1914 (when Joseph-Armand was seven years old) that Henry Ford created an assembly line that could produce an affordable car, the Model T.

Joseph-Armand loved automobiles, but he loved the engines that ran them even more. He tinkered with any engine he could get his hands on.

And not just engines. He also built his own mechanical toys. When he was fourteen he built a miniature cannon. A working cannon. He told his friends, "Watch what happens next!"

He lit the fuse.

What happened next was that the cannon exploded. With a *bang* that rocked the town. Nobody was hurt, but nobody was very pleased with Joseph-Armand, either.

Joseph-Armand didn't care—all he wanted to do was make things work (and maybe make loud noises, too).

He also wanted to invent things, and at the top of his list was inventing a machine that would go on snow. That was his second passion.

In the first part of the 20th century, most Canadian roads weren't paved—there were only dirt roads. They didn't have four or six or eight lanes—they had one, maybe two. Main roads didn't run along the outskirts of cities—they ran right down the middle of town.

But the biggest difference between then and now, at

least in snowy places, was that in the early 1900s, roads weren't plowed. No sand, no salt, no snowplow. Wherever a snowflake landed, that's where it stayed until spring.

When the snow wasn't too deep, horses could get through. There were still a lot of horses on the roads back then, especially in the countryside. But even a team of strong horses couldn't handle deep snowdrifts. They certainly couldn't trudge through thirty miles (forty-eight kilometers) of deep snow to bring a sick child to the hospital.

So folks living in very snowy places—and Joseph-Armand's town of Valcourt was one of the snowiest—hunkered down in winter. They didn't go much farther than the general store to shop or to church to pray or the woods to work. With the nearest hospital so far away, folks mostly accepted as fact or fate or God's will that there was no way to get there once the snow fell.

But not Joseph-Armand—even as a kid, he wanted to show his neighbors that they didn't have to accept this winter fate. He was obsessed with inventing a snow machine.

"Can't you see it?" Joseph-Armand asked his younger brother Léopold. "We'd be able to go wherever we want, all winter long."

"Joseph-Armand, the roads are closed in winter. Cars get stuck in half a minute."

"But *why* do they get stuck, Léopold?"

"Because their tires won't go in snow," Léopold said, rolling his eyes.

"Ah, but my snow vehicle won't have tires."

"Snow vehicle? Is that what you call it?"

"Yes, I think so."

"Well, whatever you call it, it's got to have tires. What else is there—wings?"

"I don't know yet. But someday . . . can't you just see it? Everybody in town is stuck at home, and then we come to the rescue on our snow vehicle!"

"Joseph-Armand, everybody in town thinks you're nuts. Or haven't you noticed?"

Joseph-Armand put his arm around his little brother's shoulder. "Léopold, they think that now. But . . ."

"I know, I know. When we come to the rescue on our *snow vehicle,* they'll think we're heroes. Only one thing, brother . . ."

"Yes, Léopold?"

"For now, they still think you're nuts."

CHAPTER 3
FIRST TRY

In 1922 only a few hundred people lived in Valcourt. Small towns in Quebec are like small towns everywhere—people are slow to change. The people of Valcourt weren't sure what to think about young Joseph-Armand. Especially after his cannon had boomed through their lives one year before. But Joseph-Armand wasn't about to give up his passion.

Joseph-Armand was only fifteen when he invented his first snow vehicle. In a word it was *dangerous.* Imagine the frame of an old-time sled—not a slide-down-the-hill saucer kind of sled but the horse-drawn-carriage-with-runners kind. Now, using a block and tackle to lift it, set a heavy four-cylinder Model T Ford engine near the back of the sled. Then connect the big, wooden, two-blade propeller that Joseph-Armand built to the engine. Finally, bolt everything down. Tight.

That's how Joseph-Armand built his first snow vehicle.

Joseph-Armand and Léopold pushed their contraption out of the garage and onto the snowy driveway. Joseph-Armand pulled himself up onto the sled and checked the engine settings. He pushed the spark lever up to keep the engine from kicking back. Then he opened the throttle a bit so the engine would idle once it started.

"Can I spin the prop now?" Léopold asked, standing by the propeller at the back of the machine.

"In a minute," Joseph-Armand said. He sidestepped to the front of the engine and pulled the choke wire. Returning to the back of the sled, he took a deep breath. Everything was in order. He crossed his fingers. He said a short prayer. He called to Léopold—"Ready!"

Léopold began spinning the propeller to prime the engine . . . once . . . twice . . .

"C'mon, engine," Joseph-Armand pleaded, "spark."

. . . three times . . .

Joseph-Armand gritted his teeth. "Come *on*—"

The engine coughed to life.

"CONTACT!" Joseph-Armand shouted.

Léopold raced out of the way to avoid the now whirling propeller. The sled skittered sideways as the propeller picked up speed. Joseph-Armand held on with one hand and pressed the clutch with the other.

"Léopold, hurry! Get on!"

Léopold darted to the front of the sled and jumped aboard before the machine took off on its own. He grabbed the cotton reins, ready to steer.

"The choke, Léopold," Joseph-Armand yelled over the sound of the prop. "Release the choke!"

Léopold quickly released it. "Ready!" he shouted, holding tightly to the reins.

Joseph-Armand advanced the spark lever and opened the throttle wider. One last deep breath, one last short prayer, and he let up on the clutch. . . .

With a *whoop,* the brothers and their snow machine *blazed* into the street.

Joseph-Armand and Léopold sped the roaring, weird-looking contraption through the snow-covered streets of Valcourt. They were thrilled, *thrilled!* The innocent citizens of Valcourt were . . . a little less than thrilled. Okay, a *lot* less.

The innocent citizens of Valcourt weren't the only

ones who were not amused. Joseph-Armand and Léopold's father took one look at the sled's whirling propeller, one listen to the sled's earsplitting roar, one estimate of the sled's startling speed, and said five words: "Take. That. Thing. Apart. NOW!"

"But, Papa, it worked. It *worked!*"

"God and all his saints worked. They worked at keeping my foolish sons alive."

Joseph-Armand felt a warm ray of hope in the cold winter air. "Papa, perhaps God wants us to keep working at—"

"Well, *I* want you to take this thing apart. N-O-W."

With great sadness Joseph-Armand and Léopold did as they were told. Joseph-Armand's first snow vehicle became, once again, a pile of used parts.

But at least the citizens of Valcourt now had something new to talk about.

Chapter 4
Leaving Home

"Joseph-Armand's a fine mechanic—the boy can fix anything—but . . ."

"But?"

"But he spends all his time *playing* with things."

"He says he's inventing."

"*He* says inventing—*I* say playing."

"He says he wants to invent a way to ride on snow."

"Listen, if God wanted us to ride on snow, then automobiles would have snowshoes instead of wheels. Joseph-Armand should stop this silly playing and study to become a priest, as his father wishes."

"Joseph-Armand says if priests had a way to ride on snow, they could attend the sick and dying, even in winter."

"Kindly stop telling me what Joseph-Armand says. He's only a boy, and a foolish one at that."

• • •

Small towns can be tight places for teenagers, especially for teenagers with ambition. Joseph-Armand now had two ambitions—to be the best mechanic in Quebec and to invent a snow vehicle that worked. While he tinkered and adjusted, tinkered and puttered, Joseph-Armand knew that in order to become the best mechanic that he could be, he would one day have to leave Valcourt.

He also knew that his father wouldn't permit it.

So one morning in 1924, when he was seventeen, Joseph-Armand woke before dawn, crept downstairs, left a note on the kitchen table, and slipped out the door.

We don't know exactly what the note said, but it probably went something like this:

Chers parents,

This is hard for me, and I know it will be hard for you. I must leave home—leave Valcourt—at least for now. My dream is to become the finest mechanic in Quebec. I cannot achieve that dream here. I need more knowledge and more training. The only place to get that is in Montreal.

That is where I have gone. All is well. I shall be careful. And I will return.

Your loving son,
Joseph-Armand

• • •

He took the early train out of Valcourt. Before noon he was in Montreal.

Montreal! Quebec's biggest city! Here people spoke English as well as French. There were even Chinese people, speaking and looking so different from anyone in Valcourt. And languages—Joseph-Armand knew the sound of English, he could figure out that the Chinese were speaking their language, but his ears couldn't discern the rest. Greek? Italian? Plus a dialect of French not spoken back home.

And there were so *many* people—more living on one block than in all of Valcourt.

Factories blew their whistles, and teams of workers trudged off to process flour or make nails. The air was filled with the smells of burning coal from the foundry, fresh-cut wood from the sawmill, and fish from the

Lachine Canal. Streetcars stuffed with people clanged their bells as they zipped along the rails. In the congested streets drivers honked their horns. It was loud. Terribly, shockingly, wonderfully loud.

Montreal: loud and big and crowded and maybe even dangerous. A mother's nightmare. A teenager's dream.

By nightfall Joseph-Armand was knocking on a door. As he waited for someone to answer, he stomped his feet to shake off the cold. Excitement bubbled inside him. He inhaled a breath that was half fear for what he'd done, half thrill for what lay ahead. As he exhaled, the door opened.

"May I help y—Joseph-Armand! Joseph-Armand Bombardier! *Mon dieu*—what are you doing here?"

He smiled his best nephew smile. "Good evening, Tante Marie. I've come here to learn."

"To learn? To learn what, Joseph-Armand? Do your parents know you're "

"To learn how to become the best mechanic in Quebec, *ma chère tante.* First thing in the morning, I'm signing up for a night course."

"But how will you support your—"

"And second, I start looking for a day job."

"But...but your parents? Do they know where you are?"

Joseph-Armand smiled a little smile. "Tante, I feel certain that they soon will."

Chapter 5
Good with Motors

Single-minded. sin·gle-mind·ed *adj*

1. with only one goal in mind

2. with the mind fixed on one task or preoccupation

Even as a teenager Joseph-Armand Bombardier was, above all else, single-minded. So he didn't spend his first morning in Montreal gaping at Morgan's or Eaton's, the great stores on Rue Sainte-Catherine. He didn't spend it staring up at the massive ships in the harbor. He didn't even wander through the strange and wonderful smells of Chinatown.

No, early the next morning Joseph-Armand signed up for a mechanics course. The first class would be held that night. As soon as he'd finished registering for class, he set out looking for work.

He stopped at a busy garage. It was a lot different from back home. A *lot* different.

Though he could tell from the wide doors that the garage had once been a stable, the building was made of brick, not wood. It was bigger than the church in Valcourt. There weren't two or three mechanics—there were ten or twelve. And while they were working, they were listening to music. *American* music—with words he'd never heard on any radio in any language!

Joseph-Armand listened in disbelief as a woman sang:

Ma, he's making eyes at me
Ma, he's awful nice to me
Ma, he's almost breaking my heart
I'm beside him—Mercy!
Let his conscience guide him!

Mon Dieu! Mon Dieu! thought Joseph-Armand.

Every minute he gets bolder
Now he's leaning on my shoulder
Ma, he's kissing me!

Joseph-Armand didn't know whether to walk out in disgust or to stick around and hear what happened next. As he was deciding, twisting his cap in his hand, the boss finally came over and spoke to him.

"And what do you want, young fellow?"

"I—I want a radio. *Non!* I want a *job.* If you please."

"As what, a floor sweeper?"

"As a mechanic." Joseph-Armand whispered the words.

"WHAT?"

Then louder, stronger, in his country accent: "I want a job, sir, as a mechanic. If you please."

"Oh, you do, do you? Well, you look a little young for a mechanic."

"I'm good with motors."

"Are you, now? We'll see about that. Boys, show this 'mechanic' to the English car." He winked at his crew. "Let's see if he can fix that!"

Joseph-Armand knew they were up to something, but he didn't know what. What he didn't know was this: The garage's chief mechanic had already spent endless hours trying to fix the car and had finally given up in disgust. They'd all tried; they'd all given up. The car's next stop was the junkyard.

Joseph-Armand took off his jacket. He rolled up his sleeves. He opened the hood.

Joseph-Armand looked at the cold, silent engine. He looked from above. He looked from below. He looked from both sides.

For a while the other men looked at him looking. They shook their heads; they snickered behind their hands. But when Joseph-Armand just silently kept on looking, they grew bored with the show. One by one they went back to their morning's work. By noon they'd forgotten all about the kid from the country.

All the men were sitting outside eating their lunch when, from inside the garage, they heard a click. A sputter. A cough. And then the roar of an engine. It sounded like—no, it couldn't be. But yes—*mon Dieu*—it sounded like the English car.

They poked their heads in the door just as the broken-down, no-good, will-never-run-again, pile-of-junk, heading-for-the-junkyard English car came driving toward them. In the driver's seat sat young Joseph-Armand Bombardier.

They ducked out of the way.

Joseph-Armand smiled a little smile. He waved a little wave.

As he drove by them, he said, "She runs good. Think I'll take her for a test drive."

The owner called after him, "Hey, kid! You're *hired.*"

• • •

Joseph-Armand was proud of his success at work and at school. His aunts and cousins? They hoped he would find a girlfriend.

"Joseph-Armand, you're young. You should get out, have fun."

"Joseph-Armand, there's a party tonight at Anne-Marie's. Wanna go with us?"

"Hey, Joseph-Armand! We're all going down to the movies on Rue Saint-Denis. Gonna see *The Rose of Paris.* Or maybe *Captain Blood.* You come, too."

But Joseph-Armand always said the same thing: *"Non, merci."* All he wanted to do was work and learn, learn and work.

One night his aunt stopped him on his way to class. "Joseph-Armand, you never have any fun. You just fix cars all day and study all night. Is that really worth every minute of your time?"

Joseph-Armand looked her in the eye. "It is to me, Tante. It is to me."

Chapter 6
Father and Son Reunion

In 1926 Joseph-Armand turned nineteen. He'd graduated from his mechanics course. He'd learned all he could from fixing cars. He'd lived in the big city. It was time to go home.

At the train station in Valcourt, Joseph-Armand's brother Léopold was waiting for him. Waiting with one simple question: "What are you doing back here?"

"I have to admit, Léopold, the answer surprises me. I never thought I'd say these words, but . . ."

"I'm waiting for the words, Joseph-Armand."

"I . . . I . . . I missed the place."

"You missed *Valcourt?* What's to miss?"

"The smell of the old pool hall. The freedom of the woods. Maman's pea soup; her maple pie. I even missed the town gossip, though most of the gossip was about me."

"Mon Dieu—there's no hope for you. You're just a country boy!"

"I'm afraid so." He clapped his brother on the back. "Glad to see you, Léopold—I missed you, too. However, dear brother, I won't let that stop this country boy from whupping you at a game of pool."

• • •

The truth was, country boy or not, Joseph-Armand had mixed feelings about being home. Would his father still try to make him become a priest? *Yes, of course,* Joseph-Armand thought. Did the neighbors still think he had his head in the clouds? *Yes, I know they do.* Was there anybody he could share his dream with, the dream to invent a machine that would go on snow? *No. Well, maybe Léopold. But no one else.*

• • •

Joseph-Armand's first question was answered the very day he came back to town. While he was in the pool hall, enjoying the familiar smells, he felt a presence enter the room. His friends stopped laughing, stopped joking, stopped looking his way. Joseph-Armand felt a sudden sense of dread. His always-steady hands began shaking.

He looked up. There in the doorway was his father. Joseph-Armand's knees started shaking, too.

With a small jerk of his head, Joseph-Armand's father beckoned him to come outside. *Uh-oh. This is it. The end of my dream. I should never have come home.*

Standing outside in the snow, Monsieur Bombardier looked his eldest son in the eye. "Still want to be a mechanic, Joseph-Armand?"

No *"Bonjour,"* no "Good to see you," no "Welcome home, son." Just a six-word question.

Joseph-Armand had a two-word answer. He looked his father in the eye. "Yes, sir."

"Not a priest, Joseph-Armand?"

"No, sir."

"You are absolutely certain of that?"

"Yes, sir."

"And nothing—absolutely nothing—will change your mind?"

"That's correct, sir."

There was a long, long pause. Finally Joseph-Armand's father spoke once more. "Well, then, I guess I'd better change mine."

"Sir? Wh-what did you say?"

"Joseph-Armand, I am going to help you build a garage. You can be a mechanic."

His father sighed. "God will have to find another priest."

Chapter 7
Enter Yvonne

When Joseph Armand opened Garage Bombardier in 1926, people started bringing their cars and tractors to him to fix. Word of his mechanical genius spread, and soon people stopped treating Joseph-Armand like a kid with his head full of dreams. The truth was that his head *was* still full of dreams. And his number-one dream was the same as it had always been—to invent a way to go on snow.

But, except for his brother, Joseph-Armand had no one to share his dream with. Until one day . . .

• • •

One day, or rather one night, Joseph-Armand met Yvonne Labrecque. They were very different people. Joseph-Armand was a mechanical genius, more comfortable with engines than people. His head was full of fan belts and spark plugs and cogs.

Yvonne was great with people and had zero interest in fan belts or spark plugs or cogs. "What is this 'cog,' you keep muttering about, Joseph-Armand? *Non, non,* don't tell me. Truly, I'd rather not know."

Joseph-Armand defined impatience—his head was bubbling with ideas he couldn't wait to turn into action. Yvonne was the picture of patience—with relatives, with neighbors . . . with Joseph-Armand. He was a fiend for work; to him, Saturdays were the same as Tuesdays—he spent them both tinkering in his garage. She knew how to balance work and family . . . and Joseph-Armand.

They were totally different people.

Of course, they fell in love.

Of course, they got married and had lots of kids.

Of course, they stayed together for the rest of their lives.

Love in a cold climate. Sweet as maple pie.

• • •

Some in Valcourt said, "You watch. Marriage is going to make a new man of our Joseph-Armand. He'll leave all that 'inventing' foolishness and settle down. Just you watch."

Those who said this didn't really understand Joseph-Armand Bombardier. He left that "inventing foolishness" for, oh, two days. Then he was right back at it. As happy as could be . . .

Until 1934. Until that cold and snowy night with baby Yvon upstairs in the crib, groaning in pain. With death hovering over the house. With Joseph-Armand pacing and muttering, "If only. If only . . ."

But the only "if only" that would come would be one Joseph-Armand created. And sadly, it did not come on that cold Quebec night. Like so many people who were sick and snowbound back then, little Yvon died at home, without a doctor, without an ambulance, without a way of getting to the hospital.

Like so many other grieving parents in snowy places back then, Joseph-Armand and Yvonne stood by, powerless to help.

Chapter 8
Snowmobile Fever and Bombardier Flu

There is nothing more horrible for parents than when their child dies. They would rather die themselves—if only it could save their child, they gladly would.

When a child dies, some parents turn to drink. Some turn to God. Some fall into a dark depression.

Joseph-Armand Bombardier turned to work. If he'd worked hard before—and he'd worked harder than anyone else in Valcourt—now he worked harder still. Days. Nights. Weekends and holidays and birthdays. He dedicated his life to creating that "if only." He would not rest—he could barely sleep—until he had invented a machine that would go on snow.

When single-mindedness doubles down, when it feeds on itself, when it's fueled by inconsolable grief, it becomes *obsession.* Joseph-Armand was no longer simply single-minded. Now he was a man obsessed. He was half-crazed with the driving obsession to build a snow vehicle that worked.

And so the Bombardier Garage was not an easy place after Joseph-Armand's son died.

"Arthur, you are late for work!"

"But, boss, I'm right on time."

"Normand! Where is that wrench? Why is your work-bench such a mess?"

"It's right here, Monsieur B. Same place it always is."

"Bertrand, how many times must I tell you to change the oil!"

"Sir, I changed it last night. You watched me change it."

But his men stuck by him. They checked bearings. They thawed frozen gas lines. They lined up drive shafts. When yet another test-model snow vehicle got stuck in a snowbank, they helped haul it out and drag it back to the garage.

Back then there were no tow trucks to haul a vehicle out of a snowbank. That left two choices: a team of horses

. . . or a team of Bombardier mechanics. If the snow vehicle was *really* stuck, sometimes it took both.

When a test model got stuck, they tore it apart to find out why, and then started over. When the next one didn't work, they tore it apart. Started over.

Try. Fail. Start over. Try. Fail. Start over. In spite of failures, stuck snow machines, and long hauls back to the garage, Joseph-Armand and his mechanics tinkered and puttered, built and rebuilt, again and again.

Sure, that's what Joseph-Armand's mechanics were paid to do, but it was more than that. They'd caught a dose of their boss's obsession. They had a serious case of Snowmobile Fever and Bombardier Flu. They wanted to—they needed to—build a machine that would go on snow.

• • •

And three sleepless years later . . . three stormy, difficult, disheartening, sometimes disillusioning years later . . . they did it.

CHAPTER 9

SNOWMOBILE!

In 1937, *Snow White and the Seven Dwarfs* was the big movie. Howard Hughes set a record by flying from Los Angeles to New York in seven hours, twenty-eight minutes. A revolutionary fabric called nylon was invented. In California they had finished building the Golden Gate Bridge.

• • •

And one cold, sunny morning in the winter of 1937, in the little town of Valcourt, Quebec, two young mechanics swung open the doors of Garage Bombardier. The rest of the crew stood outside, lined up as if waiting for a king to emerge. Everybody in town knew something was about to happen, and they weren't going to miss it. The towns-people lined up behind the mechanics. Yvonne and the children stood on a nearby snowbank, hopeful but silent.

Inside the garage Léopold checked the engine, checked the oil, checked everything he could think to check.

Joseph-Armand sat in the driver's seat, looking neither right nor left. All he saw was the snow beyond the open doors. He breathed in. He breathed out. Finally he gave an almost invisible nod to Léopold.

As the people of Valcourt whispered and wondered, from within the garage they heard a cough.

The cough died.

Then a second cough.

The cough died.

Then a third cough.

This one didn't die. This one sputtered into a hack, and the hack turned into a *hack-ack-ack-ack*. That became a rumble and a roar—a mighty roar.

Everybody in the crowd shaded their eyes, trying to peer into the darkness of the garage through the bright sunlight reflecting off the morning snow.

Through the open doors, there came a flash of black. Out roared a machine —a snow machine. A snowmobile!

GARAGE - BOMBARDIER

Joseph-Armand Bombardier drove it past his family, between the lines of loyal mechanics, through the cheering crowds, right over the snow.

He smiled a little smile. He waved a little wave. And. On. He. Drove.

Chapter 10
What Happened Next

He did it. He *did* it! All that time, all that work, all those tears, and he finally invented a machine that could float on snow.

With the help of his crew and the support of his family, Joseph-Armand Bombardier built a snowmobile that could go on snow without risking the lives of its passengers—or the neighbors. But it was a very different machine from today's snowmobiles.

Most of today's snowmobiles are two-person motorcycles that run on snow. They're used for entertainment, for going fast from here to there, for climbing steep hills, for moonlight rides, and most of all, for having fun.

In short today's snowmobiles are built for *recreation.* But Joseph-Armand built his vehicle for *transportation.* He designed it to carry doctors to patients, priests to parishioners, children to school. His snowmobile was even meant to carry the mail. Joseph-Armand was built for work, and so were his first snow machines. He built them not only to improve the quality of rural life but also to save the lives of people in snowbound communities—and that's just what those early snowmobiles did.

The very first snow vehicle—the one with the propeller that Joseph-Armand built in 1922 when he was

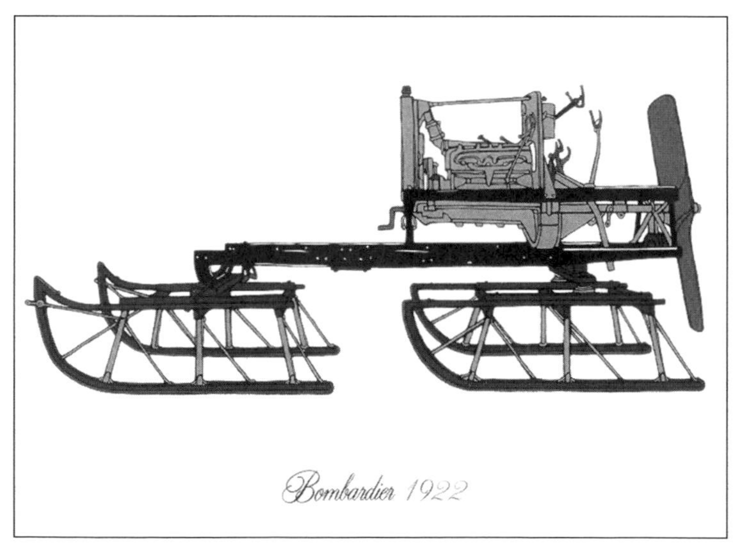

Here's a drawing of that 1922 snow vehicle.

And here's an early photo of the same vehicle sitting in the Quebec snow.

fifteen—was powered by a Model T Ford engine that Joseph-Armand had modified. The propeller, which was 4.5 feet (1.37 meters) tall, provided thrust, while Léopold provided steering via a pivoting sled runner and rope. The entire machine was 12 feet (3.66 meters) long and could probably reach a speed of thirty miles (forty-eight kilometers) per hour.

By 1937, when Joseph-Armand drove the B7 out of his garage, the snowmobile was a much more advanced machine. For one, there was no propeller—it was powered by a Ford V-8 or a Chevy 6 engine. For another, the passengers sat inside, not outside. And it was much, much bigger. Measuring 15 feet (4.57 meters) long, the B7 held seven occupants.

The 1937 B7 snowmobile

BOMBARDIER

Oh, and the name? "B" was for Bombardier; "7" for seven passengers.

But the biggest difference—the key to making it work—was a new sprocket wheel/track system. Joseph-Armand invented it in 1935 using those cogs that Yvonne didn't want to know about. He encased a cogged wheel—a.k.a. a wheel with teeth—within a rubber track. As the wheel turned the teeth turned the track and the snowmobile moved forward.

Then Joseph-Armand put two tracks, one on either side, under the back of the B7. This spread out the vehicle's weight. Now the snowmobile no longer sank in snow—it floated!

Four years later, in 1941, Joseph-Armand built the B12. It was 17 feet (5.18 meters) long and carried twelve passengers—more like a bus than a motorcycle. Due to the company's success with snow vehicles and with the military vehicles it had started building for Canada's use in World War II, the L'Auto-Neige Bombardier Limitée became incorporated the following year.

Things went well for the company for a number of years, but that changed in the late 1940s. Although people had been experimenting with snowplows as early as the 1920s, it wasn't until 1948 that the Canadian government declared that all roads be plowed in winter.

Suddenly snowmobiles weren't as important as a means of transportation. Joseph-Armand began losing money. Soon the company was nearly bankrupt.

Then in the early 1950s, Joseph-Armand came up with Plan B—the Muskeg, an all-tracked, all-terrain vehicle. Nine feet (2.74 meters) long and 5 feet (1.52 meters) wide, it was a wide-tracked snowmobile that could go over any type of terrain—desert sands, dense swamps, and treacherous mountains—thanks to its low-impact design. The Muskeg cleared roads in the Sahara. It helped skiers reach difficult slopes. Loggers used the Muskeg to work in the forests of Quebec. This all-terrain vehicle turned Joseph-Armand's fortunes around—for the better.

Joseph-Armand Bombardier and the Muskeg Tractor launched in 1953

In 1959 the switch from *transportation* to *recreation* began. That's the year that Joseph-Armand Bombardier produced his first Ski-Doo® snowmobile. The machine was only 6 feet (1.83 meters) long and 30 inches (76.2 centimeters) wide, and it weighed just 335 pounds (152 kilograms). The Ski-Doo® snowmobile was driven by a Kohler four-cycle, one-cylinder, air-cooled engine with only seven horsepower.

• • •

Although Joseph-Armand died in 1964, his memory and legacy live on. His B7 helped doctors save the lives

The 1959 Ski-Doo® snowmobile

The 2011 Ski-Doo®-MXZ 800R E-TEC is perfect for trail riders.

of snowbound patients. His B12 and C18 got snowbound children safely to school. His Muskeg brought workers into mud-soaked forests.

And today, not only does his Ski-Doo® snowmobile provide family entertainment—true to Joseph-Armand's original mission—it's also a rescue vehicle in the mountains of the world.

All this from a man who just wanted to find a way to "float on snow."

AUTHOR'S NOTE

What's real? What isn't?

I'm Jules. I wrote this book. Hi.

Let me tell you a little about it. Starting with what's real and what isn't.

What is real is every fact, every date, every person and place in the book.

What isn't real is every conversation. I read as much as I could find about Joseph-Armand Bombardier, then watched the Canadian TV series *Bombardier*, then visited the J. Armand Bombardier Museum and Valcourt, Quebec, the town where Joseph-Armand grew up.

Once I felt I knew Joseph-Armand as well as I could, I wrote the book. And invented the conversations. Truth is, nobody knows exactly what he said to his parents, his wife, his brother, his aunt, or his boss in Montreal. Nobody knows what he said in the letter to his parents when he left for Montreal. That's why I had to make it up.

But along the way, I checked the historic facts that I wrote with the J. Armand Bombardier Museum and with his family, who are very much alive and still living in Quebec.

I like to get it right, even the parts I make up.

• • •

Why did I write this story?

Two reasons . . . no, three. But one was a mistake.

So, why did I write this story?

1. I wrote it in northern Vermont, where snowmobiles are a big part of life in winter. I'm much more a skier than a snowmobiler, and most skiers hate—*hate*—snowmobiles. Not me. I like 'em. They get families outside when it's snowing; they cut trails for cross-country skiers; and they're fun, fun, fun. I've snowmobiled in Vermont, Colorado, Wyoming, even the mountains of West Virginia. I like snowmobiles.

2. In northern Vermont, whenever I'd talk at a school or library, the librarian would sigh and say, "Our boys

hate to read. Why don't you write something that they'll love to read?" That's what I've tried to do here.

3. (And this is the mistake.) Somewhere along the line, I got the idea that Joseph-Armand Bombardier invented the Ski-Doo® snowmobile because he couldn't get his dying child to the hospital in winter. That really pulled at me. It turns out that Joseph-Armand had been working on the invention since *he* was a child. The part about his son dying is true, and his death did spur Joseph-Armand to work even harder. But he was working on the dream of a lifetime, not an idea born of grief.

• • •

What's my secret dream?

Okay, I'll tell you. Here's my secret dream. . . .

I'm in an airport (I fly a lot) or in a restaurant (I eat a lot), and so are you. You're across the room, sitting with your folks. Only you're not just sitting—you're reading. And you're not just reading—you're reading a book I wrote!

It's happened once, just once. I went to a bar mitzvah in Boston, and there was somebody's younger brother, dragged along. He went without a fuss if, and only if, he could take his favorite book with him.

And yes, it was a book I wrote.

TIMELINE

1907 Joseph-Armand Bombardier is born on April 16 in the village of Valcourt, Quebec. He's the first of 8 kids; only six of them survive into adulthood.

1921 Joseph-Armand builds a cannon at 14. It works. It's dangerous. It's loud. His father is not amused.

1922 Joseph-Armand builds his first snow vehicle at 15, using an old Model T Ford engine and a homemade wooden propeller. It works. It's dangerous. It's loud. His father is not amused.

1924 Joseph-Armand takes off for Montreal. He's 17.

1926 Joseph-Armand, now 19, returns to Valcourt. He and his family build Garage Bombardier.

1929 Joseph-Armand marries Yvonne Labrecque. They have six children; five survive into adulthood.

1934 Yvon Bombardier dies of acute appendicitis. He's only two years old.

1935 Joseph-Armand invents the sprocket wheel/track system.

1937 Joseph-Armand receives his patent for the sprocket wheel/track system on June 29. He unveils the B7. That year the company sells eight of them, mainly to doctors . . . and funeral directors.

1941 Bombardier outgrows its old plant and builds a new one, the first of many yet to come. The bigger B12 is unveiled.

1942 Bombardier the company is incorporated. The company starts making military vehicles.

1945 The C18, a school bus on skis, is launched.

1953 The Muskeg, an all-terrain vehicle, is launched. Joseph-Armand receives a patent for a vulcanizing device.

1955 Joseph-Armand puts the J5 on the market; the first tracked vehicle designed specially for the forestry industry.

1956 Joseph-Armand receives a second patent for a vulcanizing device.

1959 Joseph-Armand invents the Ski-Doo® snowmobile.

1964 On February 18, Joseph-Armand Bombardier dies of cancer. He's 56 years old.

BIBLIOGRAPHY

Books about Snowmobiles and Joseph-Armand Bombardier

Bassett, Jerry. *Polaris Pioneers: A Star Is Born.* St. Paul, MN: Recreational Publications, 1989.

Coburn, Frederick S. *J. Armand Bombardier.* Montreal, QC, Canada: Joseph-Armand Bombardier Foundation, 2007. Published in conjunction with the exhibition "Frederick S. Coburn / J. Armand Bombardier: Art and Technology in the Val-Saint-François," shown at the Yvonne L. Bombardier Cultural Centre in Valcourt.

Ingham, L. Allister. *As the Snow Flies: A History of Snowmobile Development in North America.* Lanigan, SK, Canada: Snowmobile Research Publishing, 2000.

Radlauer, Ed. *Snowmobiles.* Glendale, CA: Bowmar Publishing, 1977.

Ramstead, C. J. *Legend: Arctic Cat's First Quarter Century.* Deephaven, MN: PPM Books, 1987.

Tracks on the Snow. Valcourt, QC, Canada: Musée J. Armand Bombardier, 2007.

Wood, Ted. *Iditarod Dream: Dusty and His Sled Dogs Compete in Alaska's Jr. Iditarod.* New York: Walker & Co., 1996.

TV series about snowmobiles and Joseph-Armand Bombardier

Bombardier. Canada: Telefilm Canada, 1993.

Websites

For a new take on Joseph-Armand Bombardier's original idea of using snowmobiles for *transportation*, have a look at **http://www.youtube.com/watch?v=nTDNLUzjkpg**

Visit the J. Armand Bombardier Museum. It's *so* worth the trip. **http://www.bombardiermuseum.com**

French words

bonjour: hello; good day
ma chère tante: my dear aunt
non, merci: no, thank you
mon cher: my dear
mon Dieu: my God
monsieur: mister
non: no
tante: aunt
maman: mom

INDEX

Page numbers in *italics* refer to illustrations.